TEN mantras for your SOUL

HKF Press

TEN
mantras
for your
SOUL

First printed in November 2024
Copyright © Sandipani Hume
All Rights Reserved

ISBN: 9-781838-269111

No part of this book may be reproduced, scanned or distributed in any printed or electronic form without the permission of the publisher, except in the case of brief quotations embodied in critical articles or reviews.

Published & Printed by HKF Press
Printed in the United Kingdom

हरे कृष्ण हरे कृष्ण कृष्ण कृष्ण हरे हरे
हरे राम हरे राम राम राम हरे हरे

For queries, orders, suggestions or for more information about the subject matter please contact:
sandipanihume@gmail.com

TEN mantras for your SOUL

the power of
spiritual sound

nāhaṁ tiṣṭhāmi vaikuṇṭhe
yogināṁ hṛdayeṣu vā
tatra tiṣṭhāmi nārada
yatra gāyanti mad-bhaktāḥ

I do not reside in heaven, nor in the hearts of religionists and mystics; I reside where those who call out My name with hearts full of love.

Padma Purana

ekam sad viprā
bahudhā vadanti

The Truth exists as one,
but the wise call it by various names.
Rig Veda

CONTENTS

WHAT ARE MANTRAS?

Mantras are potent ancient spiritual sounds that are chanted or meditated upon. They have properties of spiritual healing and are primarily found in the ancient Vedic texts of India and her subsequent traditions. Historically, mantras were enunciated in the Sanskrit language. They are considered a form of what is sometimes referred to as 'spiritual technology' by the people of India. Mantras have specific meanings and are often forms of prayer.

Chanting of mantras, in principle, is not an exclusive religious, ethnic, or historical practice, and the notion of higher-dimensional sound being able to affect change in matter, penetrate consciousness and the psyche of humans is a common theme in other world cultures and sciences. The term *mantra* itself can be defined as 'a sound which liberates or transports the mind'. What it liberates the mind from is a broad subject, but essentially it is from the mind's entanglement with material objects and pleasures, thereby allowing the soul's inherent expression to become manifest.

Man- (manasa): the mind. (Latin cognate: mēns. Spanish, Portuguese: Mente; French, English: mental)

-tra: (suffix) (1) an instrument (2) trāyate; to free or deliver (classical Sanskrit); cognate to the Greco-Roman root: trans (transport, move, transmit).

WHY IS MANTRA MEDITATION SO IMPORTANT?

Mantra meditation is perhaps one of the most important tools that everyone can use in their lives because everyone's needs on the deepest level are all the same. The paradox of our times is that we have greater buildings, but smaller homes. More Facebook friends, but fewer genuine real-life friendships. More changes to our lifestyle, but fewer changes in our inner development. We have advanced so much in science in the world, but we have forgotten the science of the self.

Mantra meditation is an important tool because it makes spirituality not just a faith-based, religious, or dogmatic practice but an experiential one. Therefore, it becomes akin to the empirical process in the sense that one accepts the metaphysical platform because they have experienced it. By meditation one can develop the realization that they are a soul (ātma) beyond just a body and a mind, and that the soul has a relationship with the Supersoul or the Supreme Being.

Mantra meditation is not a hobby or an activity isolated from the rest of one's life, like playing soccer or computer games, rather it is a lifestyle. Our diet, the intoxicants we consume, the words we use, and the things we watch on television all affect us. To enhance our lives, we must be very conscious of what we take in because whatever we take in directly transforms what we put out into this world.

The nature of this world is that people are generally very dissatisfied with their life, and therefore they use objects, stimulatory experiences, people, and substances to try to find a superior experience from the outer world. Unfortunately, the history of humankind shows that this approach has not succeeded, because we are looking in the wrong place.

We search outside ourselves for solutions to situations inside of ourselves, yet true resolution comes from within—and according to the yogic perspective, mantra meditation is a solution to that.

Kṛṣṇa explains in Bhagavad-gītā 2.66 that without having inner peace, where is the question of happiness? This is a very pertinent point: we are always chasing happiness, but we forget that before we plant crops on the land, we must first fertilize, nurture, and plow it. Without being in a state of *sattva-guṇa* (the mode of goodness), we cannot advance toward a truly happy life. Mantra meditation is a principal method for creating a peaceful internal environment.

Meditating with mantra doesn't need to take all day; as little as 30 minutes or even an hour each day is enough to begin. The most important thing is to give it a try and experience it for yourself. By practicing a little every day, we can begin to make a profound change in our consciousness. Rocks are among the densest and hardest objects in the world, yet over time, a steady, rhythmic drip of water—drip, drip, drip—can carve a deep impression into stone.

IS THERE POWER IN THE SANSKRIT LANGUAGE?

"The Sanskrit language, whatever be its antiquity, is of a wonderful structure; more perfect than the Greek, more copious than the Latin, and more exquisitely refined than either, yet bearing to both of them a stronger affinity, both in the roots of verbs and the forms of grammar, than could possibly have been produced by accident; so strong indeed, that no philologer could examine them all three, without believing them to have sprung from some common source, which, perhaps, no longer exists: there is a similar reason, though not quite so forcible, for supposing that both the Gothick and the Celtick, though blended with a very different idiom, had the same origin with the Sanskrit, and the old Persian might be added to this family, if this were the place for discussing any question concerning the antiquities of Persia."

Sir William Jones' speech
at the Asiatic Society, 2 Feb 1786

During the British colonial period in India, European scholars engaged linguistic experts in studying the languages of India and they became very fascinated by the Sanskrit language and the incredibly vast subject of Indology. Some prominent examples include scholars like Sir William Jones and Max Müller. European academe, fascinated by Sanskrit and its systematic structure, were inspired to formally develop the fields of linguistics and philology.

Language is often taken for granted, yet it is one of the most powerful tools on the planet. The ability to use systematic language and recursive speech are faculties particularly endowed to the human species. Our ability to communicate empowers us to transform our lives, organize ourselves efficiently, create channels for conflict resolution, and facilitate learning and education.

Sanskrit is a very important language for connecting people. Our popular contemporary languages are all derivatives or offshoots from earlier major languages. Most Europeans speak a language from the Romance, Germanic, or Slavic families. Leading linguistic scholars note that languages are interconnected, especially Indo-European languages. From an etic (outsiders) perspective, Sanskrit could be the oldest existing language based on available historical evidence. From an emic (insiders) perspective however, and according to Vedic tradition, it *is* regarded as the oldest and first language known to man.

If language is the most effective medium in which culture is spread, and Sanskrit is the oldest language in the Indo-European family, then these Sanskrit mantras or chants are not an Indian cultural phenomenon; rather, they are part of a historical Indo-European heritage and, more broadly, world culture. Sanskrit, as a shared ancestral language, has great power in unifying people. For its native speakers, it serves as the root for all contemporary languages. Just as working with a higher authority helps unify differing social groups, a common ancestral language has significant power to unify people culturally.

In Yogic and Vedic traditions, Sanskrit is the primary language of the ancient scriptures and that spoken by forms of Divinity, such as Śrī Kṛṣṇa and Rāmacandra. The enunciation of Sanskrit mantras is also believed to activate energy centers in the body, due to its special vibrations.

FORMS OF MANTRA CHANTING: JAPA AND KIRTAN

Mantra singing was popularized in the West in the 20th century by many renowned artists, such as George Harrison of the Beatles. George Harrison was one of the first Westerners to embrace Bhakti Yoga, the ancient path of devotional Yoga, and through Apple Records he released a single titled 'Hare Krishna Mantra' in 1969, as well as an album titled '*Radha Krsna Temple*'. The popularity of these songs helped bring mantra chanting and Bhakti Yoga into global awareness and the phrase "Hare Krishna" became a household word.

George Harrison: "The response that comes from chanting is in the form of bliss, or spiritual happiness, which is a much higher taste than any happiness found here in the material world. That's why I say that the more you do it, the more you don't want to stop, because it feels so nice and peaceful"[1]

[1] *Interview with Mukunda Goswami 1982*

JAPA MEDITATION

Japa is a spiritual practice prescribed in various ancient Indian texts. Since this tradition is rooted in Sanskrit, it's worth noting that "meditation" is an English term, so understanding the Sanskrit version of the word, *dhyāna,* provides better insight. *Dhyāna* derives from the root *dhī,* meaning to focus the mind.

Japa is the soft repetition of a mantra, a set number of times. This repetitive chanting with an undistracted, concentrated mind renders one into trance, allowing one to obtain direct spiritual experience. To perform Japa, one can use Japa mālā (meditation) beads. Holding each bead, using the middle finger and thumb, one can chant the mantra on one bead, and then move to the next, chant the mantra on that bead, and continue 108 times.

Unlike popular Western practices that emphasizie passivity or emptying the mind, *dhyāna* is an active, focused state. In Yogic terms, stillness arises when the mind connects (yoga) with a superior subject matter, Īśvara, rather than by trying to empty the mind artificially.

As the British Bhakti Yoga scholar and monk Tribhuvanatha das said:[4] "If you focus your mind on the inferior the result is inferior, and if you focus on the superior the result is superior. That is the principle behind Japa". Meditation (*dhyāna*) means focusing on a superior reality, and spiritual personhood is superior to a concept of simply an indistinct, impersonal energy.

In the Bhagavad-gītā 10.25, Kṛṣṇa states: *yajñānāṁ japa-yajño 'smi*: "of all spiritual practices, I am Japa". In the *Yoga Sūtras*, Patañjali states that through meditation one achieves *samādhi*, or enlightened meditation. This is achieved by stilling the waves of thoughts in the mind *(yogaś citta vṛtti nirodhaḥ [2])*. Through this process, one attains direct perception of oneself as a spiritual being *(svarūpe avasthānam [3])* and of Īśvara, the supreme being.

The Yoga Sūtras elucidate the importance of *dhyāna* and after listing different techniques, Japa is given as a superior form. In texts 1.27-29, he emphasizes 'tasya vācakaḥ praṇavaḥ'—'the sound of the Absolute Truth, Īśvara, is the sacred syllable Oṁ, and one must perform Japa to remove obstacles in one's spiritual path.' Both the Gītā and the Yoga Sūtras emphasize that by Japa one can experience spiritual reality, and ultimately Īśvara.

---

[2] *Yoga Sūtras 1.2*   [3] *Yoga Sūtras 1.3*
[4] *It is Consciousness that is Searching (HKF Press, 2020)*

KIRTAN

Kirtan differs from Japa in that it is a musical form of chanting. Harmoniums, drums, stringed instruments, and hand cymbals are common accompaniments, along with other instruments. Kirtan typically follows a 'call-and-response' structure, with a leader singing the mantra first, followed by a chorus of the whole group. Kirtan serves as a guided meditative practice through the musical chanting of mantras.

'Kirtan' (*kīrtana*) comes from the Sanskrit root '*kirt*', meaning to glorify and express love for a deity. Kirtan, simply put, is loud public chanting or glorification through chants and mantras. Kirtan is great for those interested in an authentic and traditional method of chanting, especially for the modern world. Japa is a concentrated form of dhyāna meditation, while kirtan helps to engage others and share in a group. The community form of kirtan is more precisely called *saṅkīrtana*.

Jiva Goswami, one of the eminent Vedic scholars of the medieval period, defines *sankīrtana as follows*:

bahubhir militvā yat kīrtanam
tad eva sankīrtanam
Sankīrtana is the kīrtan chanting
of a group in unison.

The root *sam* (in sankīrtana) means complete or together. It is cognate with the European roots *sum* or *syn*, as in words like *summary, synthesis,* or *symbiotic.*

japato hari nāmāni
sthāne śata-guṇādhikaḥ
ātmanam ca punāty-uccair
japan śrotṛṇ-punāti ca

Japa is surely very exalted and potent, yet *sankīrtana* is one hundred times even more powerful, as its benefits not only the chanter, but also the hearer. (Śrī Nāradīya)

LIST OF MANTRAS AND CHANTS

1. Om
2. Lokāḥ Samastāḥ Sukhino Bhavantu
3. Jai Jai Mā Kālī Kālī Mā
4. Om Namaḥ Śivāya
5. Om Namo Nārāyaṇāya
6. Sītā Rāma
7. Om Namo Bhagavate Vāsudevāya
8. Rādhe Rādhe Govinda Rādhe
9. Pañca Tattva Mantra
10. Hare Kṛṣṇa Maha Mantra

The next section will explain the meaning and wisdom of each mantra. This book adopts an inclusive approach to Vedic philosophy, while also integrating the Gauḍīya Vaiṣṇava tradition.

The Vedic tradition embraces both universalistic and specific forms of exegesis. While interpretations and perspectives always vary, this book is based on internal textual evidence rather than vernacular folk explanations in contemporary strains of Hinduism.

OM (AUM) 

This mantra is the seed of all other mantras and is described as the sound resonating throughout the ether of the universe. 'Om' is frequently highlighted in many ancient texts:

1. Om is Brahman (spiritual reality). All existence is contained within Om. (Taittiriya Upaniṣad) [5]

2. Om represents the ultimate truth. (Maṇḍūkya Upaniṣad)

3. Om is the bow, the self is the arrow, and spiritual reality is the target. As the arrow connects with the target, the soul realizes their relationship with Brahman when reciting Om. (Mundaka Upaniṣad[6])

4. Īśvara (the Supreme Being) is invoked by Om (Yoga Sūtras 1.28)

In the Bhagavad-gītā, Kṛṣṇa refers to Om in many places:

- From Om, expands spiritual knowledge. (BG 3.15)

- Of all mantras, Kṛṣṇa is personified by Om (BG 7.8)

- By uttering Om at death, one attains liberation (BG 8.13)

- Of all syllables, Kṛṣṇa represents Om. (BG 9.17)

- Since the time of creation, the 3 syllables, *Om tat sat,* have indicated Divinity; and are used in sacred ceremonies for the pleasure of Īśvara. (BG 17.23)

---

[5] *oṁ iti brahma oṁ iti idaṁ sarvam*

[6] *Mundaka Upaniṣad 2.2.4: praṇavo dhanuḥ śaro hyātmā brahma tallakṣyamucyate / apramattena veddhavyaṃ śaravattanmayo bhavet*

The Six Goswamis of Vrindavan explain AUM:[7]

a	Īśvara: Visnu, Kṛṣṇa, Rama: the masculine divinity, energetic; brahman; Bhagavan. The Lord of all worlds and living beings.
u	Śakti: Devi, Radha: the feminine divinity which provides substance and expansion; the energy; Śrī.
ṁ	Jiva: the individual living entities, parts and parcels of Īśvara.

Om reveals the Absolute Truth as non-dual (advaita), one without duality (ekaṁ advitīyam), and with an inconceivable variegatedness across three ontological categories (tattvas): Īśvara, Śakti and Jīva. We (Jīva) share in quality with the Supreme, yet differ in quantity, like a drop of sea water, compared with the vast ocean.

In science structures of matter are ultimately energy; similarly, on the spiritual plane, all forms and individual beings are ontologically composed of spiritual energy (brahman) while simultaneously maintaining their identity as forms. There is no variety outside of Brahman, but within Brahman there is variegatedness. There is an inconceivable simultaneity oneness and difference.

---

7 *a-kāreṇocyate kṛṣṇaḥ sarva-lokaika-nāyakaḥ*
u-kāreṇocyate rādhā ma-kāro jīva-vācakaḥ

LOKĀḤ SAMASTĀḤ SUKHINO BHAVAṆTU

This popular mantra focuses on peace, both for the individual and the world. Throughout the Vedic texts, the theme of peace is highlighted regularly. Sharon Gannon of Jivamukti Yoga translates the mantra as:

"May all beings everywhere be happy and free, and may the thoughts, words, and actions of my own life contribute in some way to that happiness and to that freedom for all."

Students often find it interesting how this particular mantra serves as a good example of the fact that Indian and European languages share a common ancestry:

- Lokāh: meaning 'a place' or 'location', is cognate with European words starting with the 'loc' root: location, locale, locomotion, etc.

- Sama: meaning 'complete' or 'together', is cognate with the European 'sum', 'syn', and 'homo'. Words like synthesis, summary, homogeneous.

- Sthah: meaning 'situated', has the same root as European words such as: stand, station, status, (in English); estar, estacion, este, cuesto, quello, estoy (in Latin languages).

- Sukhino: has the prefix *su* which means pleasant. It entered Greek via Persian and became the prefix eu, like euphoria, eugenics, eulogy, etc.

The first instance of this mantra is perhaps from the Upaniṣads but the first documented form is on the Inscriptions of the Rulers of the Sangama Dynasty (1336 A.D.-1485 A.D.) [8] It is said to come from a *Mangala* (auspiciousness) mantra:

> svasti-prajā-bhyaḥ pari-pāla-yantāṁ
> nyāyena mārgeṇa mahīṁ mahīśāḥ
> go-brāhmaṇebhyaḥ śubham-astu nityaṁ
> **lokāḥ samastāḥ sukhino-bhavantu**
> **oṁ śāntiḥ śāntiḥ śāntiḥ**

This is also one of the mantras chanted in the Mysore school of *Ashtanga Yoga* of K. Pattabhi Jois.

The mood of a true yogi or spiritualist is to desire the welfare of all as they share in the experience of being all spiritual, equal beings. Such people are known as *mahātmās,* great souls.

By one's work, thoughts and words, an intelligent person must act in a beneficial way for all living entities, both in this life and in the next.
(Viṣṇu Purāṇa 3.12.45)

It is the duty of every living being to perform welfare activities for the benefit of others with the life force, wealth, intelligence and words.
(Śrīmad-Bhāgavatam 10.22.35)

---

[8] *Gopal, Balakrishnan Raja (2004) Inscriptions of the Rulers of the Sangama Dynasty*

JAI JAI MĀ
KĀLĪ KĀLĪ MĀ

Kālī, the divine goddess, has many names. She is known as Durgā[9], Kālī mā, Devī, Śakti and Māyā. She is the feminine counterpart of Lord Śiva. Her three main aspects are: (1) the creative: Śakti (energy); (2) the abiding, cooperative, facilitative: Pārvatī; and (3) destructive, controlling time aspect: Kālī.

Dr Graham M. Schweig, one of the world's leading Indologists, states that Vedic theology is a form of bi-monotheism. The one supreme being has a moiety of the divine masculine and divine feminine, representing a perfect balance between the two.

The divine feminine is represented by Śrī (Lakṣmī) in the transcendent realm of Vaikuṇṭha, and she manifests as Durgā in this ephemeral realm.

The masculine aspect of God is called the energetic (śaktimān), while the feminine aspect is the energy (śakti). Śakti includes an internal and external potency, and the latter is Durgā. In later complementary texts, like the Devī Purāṇa, Durgā is even taken as the divinity and has other names to describe her grandeur. Focusing on mainstream historical Yoga and Vedanta schools of exegesis, the understanding of Durgā is derived from the

---

9 *'Durga' is cognate with European languages. "Dur" is Latin root: duro, durability, duration; meaning difficult, tough or hard) and Ga is cognate with the English 'go'. Durga means hard to escape; a fortress.*

theology presented in foundational texts such as Bhagavad-gītā and Śrīmad-Bhāgavatam. Durgā is the deity of the external potency (bahiraṅga śakti), in charge of this world on behalf of the Supreme.

She is often depicted with ten hands (symbolizing the ten forms of karma), wielding a sword to show her fierce and protective nature.

Her steed, a majestic tiger (or lion) rather than a horse, underscores her benevolent yet ferocious role as the presiding deity of the material realm.

srṣṭi-sthiti-pralaya-sādhana-śaktir ekā
chāyeva yasya bhuvanāni bibharti durgā
icchānurūpam api yasya ca ceṣṭate sā
govindam ādi-puruam tam ahaṁ bhajāmi

Māyā is the reflection of śakti in this world. She is worshiped as Durgā, the creating, preserving and destroying agency of this material world. Durgā ultimately conducts herself in accordance with Govinda, the Lord of the transcendent world.

(Brahma-samhita 5.44)

OṀ NAMAḤ ŚIVĀYA

The word *namaḥ* found in many mantras comes from the Sanskrit root 'nam', meaning to bow, or to offer respects. This root is found in the generic greetings of Indian languages: namaste or namaskār, which means 'I bow to you', or 'I offer respect unto you'. Therefore, Oṁ Namaḥ Śivāya means: 'I offer respects unto Lord Śiva'.

The name Śiva (Shiva) means auspicious. Some related include *Śambhu* (generator of auspiciousness) and *Śaṅkara* (whose activities are auspicious). Auspicious means creating an energetic environment wherein spirituality thrives.

Modern Hinduism has diverse interpretations about his ontological and theological position. According to the ancient Vedic texts, Śambhu[10] is a unique expansion of God Himself, who transforms from the original form of Viṣṇu to do a particular function within the material experience. He is not an ordinary soul (jiva) like us, but a divine being with a unique ontology. His rugged countenance and unkempt external appearance reflect his purity and detachment from vanity and possessions. His appearance is extraordinary to the layman, and therefore he is also known as 'Rudra', coming from the root 'rud' which means to shock or frighten.

---

[10] *Śambhu and Rudra are earlier names for Śiva.*

Brahma-Saṁhitā 5.45:
kṣīraṁ yathā dadhi vikāra-viśeṣa-yogāt
sañjāyate na hi tataḥ pṛthag asti hetoḥ
yaḥ śambhutām api tathā samupaiti kāryād
govindam ādi-puruṣaṁ tam ahaṁ bhajāmi

Just as milk is transformed into yogurt by a chemical agent, but still maintains a oneness while undergoing an irreversible transformation of identity from milk to yogurt, in a similar way, I revere the Supreme Govinda, whose state as Śambhu (Śiva) is a transformation for the service of destruction.

OṀ NAMO NĀRĀYAṆĀYA

Modern Hindu scholars like to emphasize the notion of a 'Hindu trinity' of Brahmā, Nārāyaṇa (Viṣṇu), and Śiva—the creator, maintainer, and the destroyer. This is taken to be only a nominative parallel to the *trinitarian* doctrine popular within Christianity, *but* a Hindu trinity cannot parallel in the sense of an ultimate theological doctrine. There is a monotheism and not a tri-theism. Edwin Bryant explains that the 'Hindu Trinity' is a post-colonial British imposition on Indic theology, as the notion of *trinity* is hinged upon the presupposition that creation of this universe is considered a *transcendent* role, but according to the ontology given clearly in systematic expositions on Vedic knowledge, such as the Bhagavad-gītā and the Purānas, creation of the universe is a material role, and the Supreme whilst giving the impetus, isn't the material creator. Therefore the only transcendent role of the three deities is that of Nārāyana; aptly named, as the transcendental refuge for living beings.

Brahmā and Śiva have a specifically functional position as *guna* avatāras, or as deities who have specific roles within the universe. In contrast, Nārāyana has a transcendent role beyond material universes. Therefore, although in one sense within the material world they have a comparatively equal role, outside of the material world, only do Nārāyana has a transcendent role.

SĪTĀ RĀMA

This chant glorifies the union of the King Rāma and His beautiful wife Sītā. They are the divine masculine and feminine, the God and Goddess in unity. India has two extremely famous epics, the Mahābhārata and the Rāmāyaṇa, which have been sung, remembered and discussed for millennia.

Many variations of **sītā-rāma** are sung, for example:

1. raghupati rāghava rāja rāma
   patita-pāvana sītā-rāma
2. sītā rāma jaya sītā rāma
   sītā rāma jaya sītā rāma
3. sītā rāma jaya jaya hanumān

Lord Rama's dearest love is His wife, Sītā. In the Rāmāyaṇa, we hear of the wonderful, enthralling and intense adventure of Lord Rāma who takes a journey to far-off lands to rescue His kidnapped wife from a very powerful demonic King Rāvaṇa who was trying to keep Her for himself. He is assisted by His brother Lakṣmaṇa, His dedicated servant Hanumān (whose form is like a divine monkey) and many other devotees, and He wins the fight against Rāvaṇa.

Being a divine Queen, Sītā keeps Her dignity and purity despite unlimited pain and trials by the demonic King Rāvaṇa. The Rāmāyaṇa is an intense epic where, due to His duties as a king, Rāma is tested to see whether He will compromise His integrity and loyalty to His citizens, or show bias towards what He personally loves.

Rāma, is also known as Rāmacandra. Many other avataras have similar names: Balarāma, Paraśurāma, Rādha Rāmana—as Rāma is a popular name. The name Rāma is defined in the Padma Purāṇa:[11]

> ramante yogino 'nante
> satyānande cid-ātmani
> iti rāma-padenāsau
> param brahmābhidhīyate
>
> Yogis take pleasure in the Supreme Self, who manifests as an absolute personal form of eternity, knowledge, and bliss. That Supreme Divinity is Rāma.

---

[11] *Padma Purāṇa – Satānāma Stotra (8) of Lord Rāmacandra*

OṀ NAMO BHAGAVATE VĀSUDEVĀYA

This well-known mantra appears in various ancient texts, and most notably in the Viṣṇu and Bhāgavata Purāṇas, the two most popular Purāṇas (ancient scriptures).

This mantra includes two names of the Supreme Being: Bhagavān and Vāsudeva. *Bhagavate* is used in the sense of calling out to the divine. *Bhaga* means great qualities or opulences, while *van* means possessor. *Vāsudeva* comes from the root *vas* meaning, 'to reside', and means that Being which pervades all things that exist. *Vāsudevāya* means 'unto Vāsudeva'.

Srimad Bhāgavatam 4.8.54: "This 12-syllable mantra is for worshiping Lord Vāsudeva. One should install the forms of the Lord, and mantra one should offer flowers and varieties of foodstuffs as a devotional offering. This should be done according to one's personal means and capability."

Viṣṇu Purāṇa:[12] Bhagavān possesses the six great qualities in superlative quantity: wealth, strength, fame, beauty, knowledge, and renunciation. Bhagavān is the Supreme Being who is completely replete with all good qualities in an unlimited quantity.

---

12 *Viṣṇu Purāṇa 6.5.47: aiśvaryasya samagrasya vīryasya yaśasaḥ śriyaḥ jñāna-vairāgyayoś caiva ṣaṇṇāṁ itī ganām bhaga*

Srimad Bhāgavatam: [13] The Supreme Being is characterized by oneness (advayam), experienced in three ways: the energy (brahman), Supersoul (Paramātmā) and as a Supreme Being (Bhagavān). [14]

Bhagavān refers specifically to the Supreme Personality of Godhead, beyond being a vague light in the sky or an abstract energy, but a transcendent personal Deity.

> Transcendental knowledge of Śrī Kṛṣṇa is deeper than the impersonal knowledge of Brahman, for it includes knowledge of not only His form and personality but also everything else related to Him. There is nothing in existence not related with Śrī Kṛṣṇa. In a sense, there is nothing but Śrī Kṛṣṇa, and yet nothing is Śrī Kṛṣṇa save and except His primeval personality.
>
> (Caitanya Caritamrita Adi 1.51, Prabhupada)

Mahābhārata[15]**:** He is called Vāsudeva in the resolution of His enveloping all creatures with the screen of illusion; or of His glorious splendour; or of His being the support and resting-place of the gods. He is called Viṣṇu because of His all-pervading nature.

---

13 Srimad Bhāgavatam 1.2.11

14 Explained further in the appendix.

[15] Mahābhārata Udyoga Parva 70
vasanāt sarvabhūtānām
vasutvād deva yonitaḥ
vāsudevas tato vedyo
vṛṣatvād vṛṣṇir ucyate

RĀDHE GOVINDA

Rādhe (Rādhā) means 'one who serves and loves the best'. She is the divine original Queen and is the topmost personification of the divine feminine. When you call out to Rādhā, you chant "Rādhe!" (in the vocative grammatical case).

Govinda is 'one who brings happiness to all souls'. *Go* means the senses, and *vinda* is 'pleasure' or 'bliss'. (In other contexts, *Go* can also refer to the land and even specifically the cows) It shares a similar meaning to the name Rāma. It is a very common name of Kṛṣṇa, the speaker of the Bhagavad-gītā.

There is a text called the Brahma Saṃhitā which outlines the glories of Govinda. He is referred to therein as *adi-puruṣam*, the original Person, the original being, the primeval conscious being.

Chanting out to Rādhe Govinda is especially powerful, as They are the source of happiness in life. For millennia in India, people have been enamored by the beautiful, youthful pastimes of Rādhā and Kṛṣṇa as they play, dance, and explore the enchanting land of Vṛndāvana. Their pure, divine love continues to inspire generations of people seeking to serve this beautiful concept of divinity, which encompasses all types of loving relationships and moods. By chanting to Rādhā Govinda we can repose our love in something superior. The nature of humankind is we try to love things of this world, whether it be objects, wealth, possessions, people, situations or positions.

Unfortunately, those things give us a flicker of pleasure, but are not profoundly fulfilling to fill the gap we have in our heart, for an unlimitedly deep loving relationship, such a relation is only fulfilled in the unlimited, the divine. That is the importance of Rādhe Govinda.

dīvyad-vṛndāraṇya-kalpa-drumādhaḥ-
śrīmad-ratnāgāra-siṁhāsana-sthau
śrīmad-rādhā-śrīla-govinda-devau
preṣṭhālībhiḥ sevyamānau smarāmi

In a temple of jewels in Vṛndāvana, underneath a desire tree, Śrī Śrī Rādhā-Govinda, served by Their most confidential associates sit upon an effulgent throne. I offer my humble obeisances unto Them.

(Caitanya-caritāmṛta Ādi 1.16)

PAÑCA TATTVA MANTRA

śrī-kṛṣṇa-caitanya
prabhu nityānanda
śrī-advaita gadādhara
śrivāsādi-
gaura-bhakta-vṛnda

The recent revival of Kīrtan began with these five saints and avatars in India who appeared in the 15th century. They repopularized the spiritual pilgrimage sites of Mayapur and Vrindavan and spread the chanting of sacred mantras to bring peace, prosperity, and spiritual blessings throughout India.

To achieve a profound spiritual effect in kirtan, Indian traditions always perform an invocation to the previous saints and sages to empower one's practice. Therefore, this mantra is highly recommended for learning, as it empowers one's mantra chanting by

invoking the important avatāra(s) related to kirtan.

Almost akin to the patron saint of kīrtan, Śrī Kṛṣṇa Caitanya is described as an avatāra of Kṛṣṇa, and He shared newer depths of the process of Saṅkīrtana and Bhakti Yoga throughout India, and He predicted it will soon spread all over the world. He composed one of the most eloquent poems, rich in theology and spiritual insight, called the Śikṣāṣṭakam (the 8-verse prayer of spiritual instruction).

His poem opens with the analogy, *ceto-darpaṇa-mārjanam*, that chanting Hare Kṛṣṇa has an effect equal to cleansing the mirror of the heart so one can see the beauty of the soul, and let its grace and divine qualities shine through once again. The third stanza of the poem is very beautiful:

tṛṇād api sunīcena
taror api sahiṣṇunā
amāninā mānadena
kīrtanīyaḥ sadā hariḥ

To make the full effect of kirtan, one must chant with a heart as humble as a blade of grass, with tolerance comparable to that of a tree, giving respect whilst never expecting it for oneself, in such a state of mind one can make one's life an offering of kirtan always.

HARE KṚṢṆA MAHĀ MANTRA

The ancient *Yajur Veda* recommends the *hare kṛṣṇa* mantra (Kālī-santarana Upaniṣad):

> iti ṣoḍaśakaṁ nāmnāṁ
>
> kali-kalmaṣa-nāśanam
>
> nataḥ parataropāyaḥ
>
> sarva-vedeṣu dṛśyate
>
> The sixteen names of the Hare Kṛṣṇa mantra destroy all the inauspiciousness of the age of Kali Yuga (the current age). This is the conclusion of all the Vedas. This is the most recommended mantra in within the Vedas, as a remedy for this difficult age.

Any individual has the right to choose what medicine they want to take, but ideally one should seek a prescribed treatment from a qualified doctor. Similarly, we may choose any mantra, but this mantra serves as a prescription for Kali Yuga. The three primary names in this mantra are Hare, Kṛṣṇa, and Rāma.

Hare has a twofold meaning grammatically, referring either to Hari (the supreme masculine) or Hara (the supreme feminine). When modified in the vocative case, both names become Hare, thus, it can signify either Kṛṣṇa or Rādha. This mantra is traditionally chanted by Gauḍīya Vaiṣṇavas. Caitanya Mahāprabhu, the foremost proponent of this mantra during the medieval times, and his disciples, the six Gosvāmīs of Vrindavan, explain that at the highest understanding, this mantra refers to Rādharani. The Vedas elucidate that the moiety of divinity, being both masculine and feminine is indivisible (śakti-śaktimator abheda).

Kṛṣṇa comprises two components: *kṛṣ* and *na*. Kṛṣ means attraction (karṣati). Kṛṣṭi means to pull something or attract one's attention. The second component, *na*, derives from the root *'nand'* which means happiness, *ānanda* is the same word with a prefix to intensify it into meaning divine bliss. This name is often regarded as the principal, if not the ultimate name for Bhagavān, as it embodies the essence of all His qualities. Nothing in existence is more attractive, compelling or intoxicating than experiencing vision of Bhagavān, the all-attractive.

Rāma means 'the reservoir of pleasure', or 'the source of happiness'. Many Viṣṇu Avatāras have the name Rāma in their name: *Balarāma, Paraśurāma, Nityānanda Rāma*. But this *Rāma* is the name of Kṛṣṇa as Rādhā-Ramaṇa, one who gives happiness and love to Rādhārāṇī. As Rāma comes from the root *'ram'*, meaning 'delight', this name emphasizes that God is not only a spiritual energy but He is a personal transcendent deity, who has splendorous activities on the spiritual plane. Therefore the name doesn't just signify happiness, but delight, derived from *līlā:* or divine play and recreation. Thus, the name Rāma has deep theological meaning, strongly emphasizing that *lila*, or the personal loving pastimes as God as a personal being are amongst His topmost qualities.

As shared earlier, Om is considered to be the seed of all transcendental sound. However, Bhaktas prefer names of Bhagavān, such as Kṛṣṇa and Rāma even more than Om, since Bhakti (love) is in the details—the personal name and form of Divinity. Om is the seed, and names like Kṛṣṇa are like the fruit of the tree; the seed is important, but the real beauty and sweetness come from the fruit.

harer nāma harer nāma
harer nāmaiva kevalam
kalau nāsty eva nāsty eva
nasty eva gatir anyathā

In this age of quarrel and hypocrisy, the only means of spiritual upliftment is the chanting of God's Names. There is no other way. There is no other way. There is no other way. (Bṛhan Nāradīya Purāṇa)

APPENDICES

RECOMMENDED ARTISTS TO HEAR MANTRA / KIRTAN

Of course, in this world there are thousands of wonderful kirtan artists, these are some who have shared mantra very widely:

1. Srila A.C. Bhaktivedanta Swami Prabhupada
2. Jahnavi Harrison
3. Gaura Vani & As Kindred Spirits
4. Achyuta Gopi
5. Bada Haridas
6. Radhika das
7. Amala Harinam
8. Kadamba Kanana Swami
9. GoKirtan
10. Shelter
11. MC Yogi
12. Kirtan Premi
13. Karnamrita
14. The Kirtaniyas
15. George Harrison

DIFFERENTIATING BETWEEN MANTRAS, CHANTS AND NAMA

In maintaining consistency within the tradition, the usage of *mantra* can encompass both its broader English definition and its technical Sanskrit usage. Therefore, the reader should use their discretion to determine which definition is applicable in each context.

Mantra can both mean both a general 'repetitive chant'—or a strictly private mantra, to be recited very quietly and only received in religious ceremonies. Mantra more broadly is also defined as chants that can be chanted in public and are used in kirtan and spiritual recitals. In this book, both of these definitions have been used. A traditional distinction between mantra and nāma (chants) is clarified by Bhaktisiddhānta Sarasvatī:

> Any mantra that starts with a bīja (aum, klīm, etc.) and ends in the dative case (kṛṣṇāya, vāsudevāya, śivāya) should not be chanted loudly. But nāma, or the vocative form of names, as well as mantras that do not include bīja or oṁ and which end not in the fourth [dative] case but with the word namaḥ can be chanted loudly. For example, "haraye namaḥ kṛṣṇa-yādavāya namaḥ" is chanted loudly.
> (Commentary to Caitanya-bhāgavata Madhya, 23.81)

WHAT IS ŚABDA (SOUND)?

The Vedic ontology of sound, defined as:

> arthāśrayatvaṁ śabdasya
> draṣṭur liṅgatvam eva ca
> tan-mātratvaṁ ca nabhaso
> lakṣaṇaṁ kavayo viduḥ
> (Srimad Bhagavatam 3.26.33)

1) that which conveys the idea of an object;
2) indicates the presence of a formator of sound;
3) constitutes the subtle form of ether.

Bharthṛhari, a great Sanskrit grammarian, states:

> *vāk eva viśvā bhuvanāni jajñe*
> Sound (vāk) is that element in
> which the worlds are created from. [16]

According to the Vedic perspective, all objects which manifest within the Universe are originally created by sound: "*artha-sṛṣṭeḥ pūrvaṁ śabda-sṛṣṭiḥ* ". This is taught in the philosophy of Sāṅkhya.

One of the most essential scriptures on metaphyics explains that "tat-pūrvakatvād vacaḥ": sound has existed before the material creation and that by spiritual sound itself can material entanglement be remediated (**anāvṛttiḥ śabdāt**)[17]. (Vedānta-sūtra)

---

[16] *Vakyapadiya 1.112*
[17] *Freedom from vritti is also the goal in Patañjali's Yoga system and mantra is the same cure he recommends.*

RECEIVING MANTRAS FROM A GURU?

Just as a qualification or certificate is awarded to a party upon becoming qualified, mantras are imparted by a spiritual master to a disciple. Despite modern Western yoga trends, mantras are not mystical consumer products, even though many schools charge for memberships, secret mantras, initiations, or ceremonies.

In India, there's an analogy that a delicate ripe mango is not thrown from the tree. Instead, it is gently passed hand to hand, from higher branches to the ground. Similarly, mantras have been carefully passed down for generations from guru to disciple (the paramparā system). The potency of a mantra lies in its lineage, not just its external sound.

Once Prabhupāda shared with George Harrison and John Lennon that, out of compassion for those suffering from spiritual deprivation, a great teacher, Madhvācārya, publicized a secret mantra, despite the consequences of disobedience to his guru and negative reactions. His selfless compassion moved his own guru, who, in acknowledging Madhvācārya's greatness, said to his disciple, "Now you are *my* guru."

Mantra meditation should be shared for the benefit of everyone, but one also should receive it from a *bona fide* guru in order to chant with a proper divine connection.

THE DEEPER MEANING OF BHAGAVAN

Bhagavān is one of the most common words for the divinity, God, the Supreme Being, and the creator. It is also a technical philosophical term and an important nomenclature that denotes the scripturally authorized way of harmonizing the varied descriptions of Brahman in the various Vedic, Purāṇic, and Tantric texts.

Brahman is experienced as the non-dual, nirguṇa (without variety) impersonal form of the supreme, pervading everything, that everything is one in quality.

Paramātmā reveals that ultimately, Brahman is present in a localized, more personal form: the Supersoul. He resides in all atoms and in the hearts of all living beings, providing guidance, intuition, instinct, and inspiration.

Bhagavān shows that although God is one with everything, He simultaneously maintains a distinct, personal, limitless, transcendental form and abode called Vaikuṇṭha. Kṛṣṇa and His energy are non-different and yet the energy is not Kṛṣṇa.

> Learned souls refer to the non-dual Absolute Truth in three ways: Brahman, Paramātmā or Bhagavān.
> (Śrīmad-Bhāgavatam 1.2.11)

A DEEPER EXPLANATION OF HARE KṚṢṆA

This transcendental vibration, by chanting of:

Hare Kṛṣṇa Hare Kṛṣṇa Kṛṣṇa Kṛṣṇa Hare Hare

Hare Rama Hare Rama Rama Rama Hare Hare

…is the sublime method for reviving our Kṛṣṇa consciousness.

As living spiritual souls, we are all originally Kṛṣṇa conscious entities, but due to our association with matter from time immemorial, our consciousness is now polluted by the material atmosphere. In this polluted concept of life, we are all trying to exploit the resources of material nature, but actually, we are becoming more and more entangled in her complexities. This illusion is called māyā, or hard struggle for existence for winning over the stringent laws of material nature. This illusory struggle against the material nature can at once be stopped by the revival of our Kṛṣṇa consciousness.

Kṛṣṇa consciousness is not an artificial imposition on the mind. This consciousness is the original energy of the living entity. When we hear the transcendental vibration, this consciousness is revived, and the process is recommended by authorities for this age. By practical experience also, we can perceive that by chanting this mahā-mantra, or the great chanting for deliverance, one can at once feel transcendental ecstasy from the spiritual stratum.

When one is factually on the plane of spiritual understanding, surpassing the stages of sense, mind, and intelligence, one is situated on the transcendental plane. This chanting of Hare Kṛṣṇa, Hare Kṛṣṇa, Kṛṣṇa Kṛṣṇa, Hare Hare, Hare Rāma, Hare Rāma, Rāma Rāma, Hare Hare is directly enacted from the spiritual platform, surpassing all lower status of consciousness, namely sensual, mental, and intellectual.

There is no need of understanding the language of the mantra, nor is there any need of mental speculation, nor any intellectual adjustment for chanting this mahā-mantra. It springs automatically from the spiritual platform, and as such, anyone can take part in this transcendental sound vibration without any previous qualification and dance in ecstasy. We have seen it practically. Even a child can take part in the chanting, or even a dog can take part in it.

This chanting should be heard from the lips of a pure devotee of the Lord so that immediate effect can be achieved. As far as possible, chanting from the lips of a non-devotee should be avoided, as much as milk touched by the lips of a serpent causes poisonous effect.

The word Harā is a form of addressing the energy of the Lord. Both Kṛṣṇa and Rāma are forms of addressing directly the Lord, and they mean "the highest pleasure eternal." Hara is the supreme pleasure potency of the Lord. This potency, when addressed as Hare, helps us in reaching the Supreme Lord.

The material energy, called māyā, is also one of the multi-potencies of the Lord, as much as we are also a marginal potency of the Lord. The living entities are described as a superior energy compared to matter. When the superior energy is in contact with the inferior energy, it becomes an incompatible situation. However, when the supreme marginal potency is in contact with the spiritual potency, Harā, it becomes the happy, normal condition of the living entity.

The three words, namely Harā, Kṛṣṇa, and Rāma, are transcendental seeds of the mahā-mantra, and the chanting is a spiritual call for the Lord and His internal energy Harā for protecting the conditioned soul. This chanting is exactly like the genuine cry of a child for its mother. Mother Harā helps the devotee achieve the grace of the Supreme Father, Hari or Kṛṣṇa, and the Lord reveals Himself to the devotee who chants this mantra sincerely.

Therefore, no other means of spiritual realization is as effective in this age of quarrel and hypocrisy as the chanting of the mahā-mantra.

- His Divine Grace A.C. Bhaktivedanta Swami Prabhupada

SANSKRIT PRONOUNCIATION GUIDE

As you have seen in this book, different symbols and characters have been used with the general English letters to facilitate the proper representation of Sanskrit sounds. This book uses the transliteration characters from the IAST standard. Below is a guide on how to pronounce those characters:

VOWELS

- a as in but or cup

- ā as in balm or calm

- i as in sit or hit

- ī as in feet or meet

- u as in put or pull

- ū as in mood or dude

- e as in wait or hate

- o as in home or rome

- ṛ as in r in curd or bird, and the ri in cricket. *(pronounced with the tongue bend backwards and up.)*

DIPTHONGS (DOUBLE VOWELS)

- ai as in aisle or high

- au as in how or cow

CONSONANTS

- c as in mu**ch** or su**ch** *(a **ch** sound, not a **k** sound)*

- s as in **s**ave or **s**ight

- ś as in **sh**ave or **sh**ine

- ṣ is pronounced like ś, but the tip of the tongue is bent backwards slightly. *(Not common in English)*

- t, d, n are pronounced with the tip of the tongue against the top teeth.

- ṭ, ḍ, ṇ are pronounced with the tip of the tongue bent back slightly to touch the roof of the mouth.

- ph as in u**p**hold or to**p h**eavy *(an aspirated **ph**. not like **ph**oto)*

- th as in po**th**ole or bu**t h**e *(not like **th**at, **th**ink or **th**ey)*

- ṁ isnt the consonant m, but is produced like a nasalization of a previous vowel.

- ṅ as in i**n**k or si**n**g (a velar nasal sound).

- ñ as in ca**ny**on or o**ni**on.

- jñ as in **gnya**. Like **gun-y**ellow without the *u*

- r is a rolled r, as in Spanish *prisa*.

- v is a soft v as in **v**ery or sa**v**e *(unless in clusters like t**v**am, it becomes like a soft **w**)*

- ḥ echoes the last vowel; nama**ḥ** would be nama**ha**

SUGGESTIVE QUESTIONS TO JOURNAL ABOUT AFTER MEDITATION

How did I feel after meditating, both physically and emotionally today?

How easy was it to control my mind? Did It wander a lot or a little?

What is one intention or prayer I can hold on to whilst meditating?

What are some habits I wish to overcome through meditation and strengthening the mind?

NOTES

www.ingramcontent.com/pod-product-compliance
Lightning Source LLC
Chambersburg PA
CBHW050018040726
47599CB00014B/1447